Do I have a
Guardian Angel?

SELENA HILL

BALBOA.
PRESS

A DIVISION OF HAY HOUSE

Balboa Press books may be ordered through booksellers or by contacting:

Balboa Press
A Division of Hay House
1663 Liberty Drive
Bloomington, IN 47403
www.balboapress.com.au
1-(877) 407-4847

ISBN: 978-1-4525-0630-2 (sc)
ISBN: 978-1-4525-0631-9 (e)

Printed in the United States of America

Balboa Press rev. date: 07/17/2012

For
my husband, Trent, and my four
gorgeous babies,
Charlie, Ethan, Keiley, and Chase—
xxxxx

CONTENTS

ACKNOWLEDGEMENTS

I would like to start, first of all, by acknowledging my parents, who never stopped loving me, even after the storm I created for us. I also send my gratitude to Katie: thanks for always just being there, especially during my period of self-discovery, and for always caring. To Tracey Stoppard, for throwing me in the deep end—lucky I could swim! And of course, to my husband, for always allowing me to run with my dream and supporting me the whole way. My babies, I hope that by always knowing your angels, you can avoid doing things the hard way. Thanks, angels, for every day you bring me peace. I am very grateful to be of service, to help others to have peace in their lives also.

I have written this book to showcase the miracles that angels preform for everyday people every day. It is my wish that by sharing my life with the world, people will jump on board and spend time chatting to the angels, who are just standing around doing nothing until we open our hearts to them.

INTRODUCTION

I began my life's journey without the knowledge that angels existed. As a child, I prayed every night for God to bless and look after everyone in my life, while I secretly feared death and ghosts. I lived in constant fear that someone was in my room, and I had no idea how to deal with this, other than hiding under the sheets at night. Not until my life hit rock bottom as a young adult, with illness and a loveless marriage, did I start looking into other ways to make myself feel happy. Through this journey, I have been able to be of service to hundreds of people, by way of psychic readings and healings that I preform on a regular basis with the assistance of angels. I have so many miracles in my life that I was guided to write this book so other people can learn what a difference angels can make in our lives.

Without the knowledge of angels, we sometimes feel all alone and unloved, but that never needs to be true. We all have guardian angels that can help us with even the smallest requests. I have written about events in my life as I see true. I hope you will have many angel miracles too. I've had so many angelic interventions that I can't possibly share them all. For the purposes of this book, I am including just the experiences that saved or changed lives, but this is by no means all of them. I would love for everyone to take my experience to make his or her life one of joy, which is what I now experience each and every day.

THE BEGINNING

My spiritual journey began in my late teens. I was diagnosed with rheumatoid arthritis and had to take a steroid medication with many side effects for the rest of my life. Life was very stressful at this time, and I would visit psychics on a regular basis to seek direction. One of them suggested Reiki.

Reiki is a universal life-force energy, an energy that is in everything. The Reiki practitioner channels the energy through the top of the head—known as the *crown chakra*—and the energy goes through to the heart chakra and out the palms of the hands. The practitioner simply places his or her hands on the client for the energy to be transferred. It is a very gentle and loving energy. Reiki is rumoured to have been used by Jesus with his "laying on of hands," though the practice predates even him. This ancient healing technique has three levels and can be learnt by anyone of any age. The attunement process is handed from teacher to student. The attunement simply opens one's chakras so they can hold the Reiki energy and pass it to another.

After the psychic reading, I immediately arranged for a treatment from someone I knew. After a healing session with her, I went on my own adventure and sourced a Reiki teacher. I was quick to get an attunement and take control of my own healing. Within a few days of this attunement, I began to wean myself off of all the drugs. Today, I have no sign of the rheumatoid arthritis; it has been well over a decade now. After one of the attunements, my tongue—which I had previously bitten repeatedly in the same spot—healed by the time I got home, like there had never been a cut there. Within a short period of time, I mastered all three levels of Reiki and became a teacher. I began the mission to heal the world.

On my spiritual path, I learned that thought patterns create the diseases we have. Reiki has a very loving and gentle way of showing us this. When combining angels and Reiki, miracles constantly take place. With the attunement came a lot of my psychic gifts; the more I used Reiki, the stronger these gifts became. Reiki attunements open and cleanse our chakras.

Everyone has seven major chakras. *Chakra* is a word from the ancient Sanskrit language meaning *wheel*. When these "wheels" become dirty through negative thoughts, beliefs, drugs (both medicinal and recreational), alcohol, and unhealthy foods, the chakras become clogged; the spinning fan within the chakras slows down or stops and then creates imbalances within the body called "diseases."

My psychic gifts had always been there, but because of my fears, I had shut them out of my life. Then I began hearing and seeing things. I had not experienced this before. This excited me. I began chatting to anything I came in contact with that said it was my guide or angel. Your Reiki teacher should teach you to protect yourself before every Reiki session, whether it is for yourself or others. I was unaware of the Archangel Michael, or any method of protection. I was a free-for-all, light and dark forces. So whenever I teach Reiki, psychic, or mediumship classes, protection is always my top priority. I also ensure that my students understand the messages our bodies tell us when a spirit is not authentic.

I had some very hairy experiences. Once, my car was pulled over to the side of the road and turned off and then would not start. I just kept asking angels to help me. The car started, and off I drove. I've had the phone ringing constantly with no one there. I would hear the kitchen cupboards being emptied, with things smashing all over the floor, but when I went to look, nothing had happened. I rang another Reiki master for help, and she put a triangle of protection around me and my home. My newfound Reiki master also gave me the details of a lady who removed "entities." The entity remover took more than nine hundred lower energies from my home. Apparently, my home used to be a party house; no wonder some crazy stuff was going on!

Whenever we are angry, exchanging hurtful words with someone, experiencing fear, or drinking or taking drugs, we leave part of our energy behind. This energy takes on a life force of its own. The energy we leave behind has a built-in memory of the action that took place. The energy—or entity, as it is commonly known—gets increasingly stronger when it can latch itself onto us. This is what was happening in my home, car, and place of work.

Rest assured that this is not a regular occurrence for people who receive the Reiki attunement. My experience happened simply because I had not been taught how to keep myself safe. This was a great lesson for me; the information I now have on protection is priceless, and I can pass it on to many others.

I spent a lot of time chatting with my angels, asking them for help in my life. I was very sad, and I was in a relationship where I thought that by showing someone love, I could fix them. The number one lesson: you can't heal anyone who does not want to be healed. This is a major lesson for all of us light workers. Unless someone is willing to change, we can't do the work for them, no matter how hard we try. During this time, I got married and had two lovely children. It was with these two gifts from God that I grew very strong. I constantly asked the angels to fix my partner, but of course, this never occurred. I was looking for the white picket fence in the wrong place.

Another lesson I learned is that you simply need to tell the angel what the problem is and get out of the way. By telling the angels how I thought the situation should be fixed, it stopped them from doing their work. As I only had eyes for the way I thought it should be fixed, I was missing their messages of removing myself from the situation. I ignored the feelings in my body.

Of course, if you have a child with someone, you may feel that you owe it to your child to give him or her both a mother *and* a father. None of us goes into marriage thinking that we will get divorced someday. No matter what the parents may dish out, we want a family for our children. In truth, you are teaching the child that it is okay to be unhappy and to go without a loving relationship.

As parents, we only want the absolute best for our children. It is important for us to take charge and show our children that we all deserve to be happy. Ultimately, what is right for you is right for your children. It takes courage and strength to remove yourself from such a relationship, but the rewards always outweigh an unhappy life. If you're not happy, is your child happy?

Almost the instant my second child was born, I stumbled across Doreen Virtue and her angel books. *Messages from the Angels* was the first book I read. I was very excited to find these books; who knew anything like this even existed? I then went on to read Doreen's book, *Light Workers Way.* I had a constant hunger for knowledge. I read a couple of Doreen's books each day. I instantly started using all the tools Doreen had taught in her books in my life. It was from her teachings, through these books, that I grew my psychic abilities and a deep relationship with my guardian angels and the archangels. The archangels are very strong guides in my life and have brought many blessings to my family and me.

I instantly began giving psychic readings to my friends and family. I could clearly see, hear, and feel the presence of angels. When I began passing on the angels' messages, I gave my friends and family members everything I felt, everything I heard, everything I saw. This vision appeared inside my mind a bit like a dream. I also relayed everything I felt. The feeling comes hand in hand with a vision; it helps me to understand what the angels are showing me. When information comes through as a strong knowingness, I pass that on too. I give everything over, not holding on to any piece of information.

I notice that it may not make sense to me, but it does to the person I am reading for. Prior to this newfound knowledge, I would receive messages from guides and angels while giving a Reiki treatment. Images were given to me inside my head regarding what was going on in that person's life or issues they may be struggling with. I also feel the pain of the person on the table. When I receive this information, it helps me to know where the client needs healing. Reiki gave me the courage to give psychic readings, as I had been doing mini-readings during my Reiki healings.

One day, while sharing lunch with my mother, I saw her father standing behind her. Bear in mind that he had been dead for about twenty years. She has a photo of him, and that is the only way I know him to look; I was quite young when he passed. He appeared to me exactly the way he looked in this photo, over my mother's shoulder. I thought at first that I was seeing things, so I continued to eat lunch. But he persisted; every time I looked at my mother, there he was.

Talking with deceased people is not something I was comfortable doing, nor had I noticed any of them previously. The whole idea scared me. I closed my eyes and opened them again; he still stood directly behind her. I felt a sudden push to let Mum know he was there. As soon as I said, "I am sure I can see your dad standing behind you," my mother was quick to reply, "It is funny you say that. The knobs on the stove keep turning on. I wondered if it might be him."

With that, I began channelling information from her childhood. He said, as clearly as I can hear any living person, "Tell her I know she used to keep the light on for me."

I repeated my grandfather's statement to my mother, and she instantly began to cry. "Nobody knows that," she replied.

He asked for her forgiveness. He had been an alcoholic, and my mother grew up without him. I have found that forgiveness is one of the main reasons deceased people want to get in contact with their loved ones. Then he said, and I reiterated, "I have to go now. I am going to be reincarnated as Selena's third child; a daughter." With that, I saw him walk with a massive angel behind him up white stairs that just kept going all the way to heaven. Yes, my third child is a daughter, but it was three years later that she was conceived.

It was a very emotional time for my mother, and a lot of grief was lifted. However, the day had only just begun. My mother and I had been in a back room of her house. We ventured back out to the lounge, where I could see— as clearly as you and me—her deceased brother, my uncle, sitting at the dining room table. He too began giving me messages, so I could give them to my mother. I could see him and hear his voice just as if he were still alive. My mother was excited about his being there and began chatting rather than listening. He even made a joke about how my mother loves to chat. As I passed along his messages, I felt like I had been doing this forever.

I was instantly taken back to a past life and shown things with my physical eye. I felt like I was in ancient Egypt. I had an overwhelming feeling of love for being a medium during this Egyptian life. In this past life, I felt and saw that I was a very powerful communicator of spirit, a priestess. I also wore a lot of expensive jewellery. I was well respected for the work I did. This experience lasted for only a couple of minutes, but the impact on my psychic work was very profound. It anchored me into my work by giving me a knowledge that I need to pursue the mediumship and psychic activities.

Right after my past-life experience, it came time for my uncle to leave. His exit was not as dramatic as my grandfather's; he just disappeared. The air felt empty, and I could no longer see him. My uncle's presence was purely to help me feel safe and comfortable being a medium. Of course, at the same time, it gave my mother closure to know that he was at peace.

Just as I thought I was done, another deceased man I did not recognise was standing at my mother's front door. As I did not know him, I had to describe a lot of the sensations he was giving me. At first I had trouble speaking and felt like I had problems with my throat. The deceased man was showing me how he was feeling when he was alive. These sensations were backed up by feelings. I felt that his throat had something to do with the cause of his death. From this information, my mother knew he was one of her uncles, a man named Percy, who had died of throat cancer.

He too had great insights for my mother. Percy lectured her on smoking, saying that this was the cause of his painful death. When he had passed on all of his information, the air changed. Again the air felt as though it was just emptied.

The next day, when I went to see my mother, I could hear all of her thoughts. I was telling her everything she was thinking. This did not last for too long, for which I am grateful! My mother was the catalyst I needed to take my newfound gift out into the real world.

This experience led me to the beginning of my career. My first job as a psychic medium was at a psychologist's office. My ex was seeing a psychologist and mentioned my psychic readings to her, as she was quite spiritual herself. She was very interested in having me give readings and preform Reiki at her practise. I had my own room and ran my business from there couple of days a week. My children were quite young, and this was the amount of time I was comfortable being away from my babies.

The psychologist would regularly send me her clients, to pass on some psychic insight. One of the first times I recognised being of service was when a young girl and her mother came to see me. The young girl was having a lot of trouble in school. Her mother could never get her to school, and the young girl had no friends. They wanted to know if there was a school they could take her to where she would have friends and love to go. The angels instantly showed me, in my mind's eye, a small school next to a vacant lot. I was able to describe in great detail the characteristics of the school. Her parents went looking for the school; her mother had written down everything as I said it, and they found it! The school was exactly as I described it and was a comfortable distance from their home.

I did not see the young girl or her family again. However, that Christmas I received a card from the family. Her mother wrote that her daughter had settled in very well at the new school and had lots of friends and a great teacher. She went on to say that the girl's achievements were too many to mention, but she named a few, such as the readers' cup and playing the cello in the school band. They even popped in a photo of her at QEII, representing her school. She was very grateful to have a child who was now eager to go to school.

As I read this card, tears of joy streamed down my face. This is exactly how I wish to be of service to many more. I felt very blessed to be able to pass on the messages of angels. I still have this card; it sits proudly on top of my desk with other thank-you cards I have received over the years. I feel very blessed to be the channel through which others can hear their angels' or loved ones' messages.

DO I HAVE A
GUARDIAN ANGEL?

I have been a professional psychic medium since 2004. In that time, I have done thousands of readings. One question I am regularly asked is, "Do I have a guardian angel?" My answer is always "Yes." A lot of my clients ask whether these guardian angels are a mother, brother, father, uncle, aunty, friend, and so on.

Our deceased loved ones are with us and others we love. They may have wings and give us loving guidance. Sometimes they work with angels to help us along on our life's journey and can ensure that a miracle can happen for us. However, they are not your guardian angels.

Our guardian angels are with us from our conception through our entire lifespan, and they will even be there when we cross over. Every person has at least two guardian angels. The difference between departed loved ones and angels is that angels have never been on Earth as humans and therefore have no ego. These celestial beings are here to assist us in making decisions. They will never leave you.

Angels come in an array of different sizes, shapes, and colours. I see guardian angels as being larger than us. I have seen them in totally bright white and as small lights appearing above someone's head. Once, when looking at my son, Ethan, I saw six different-coloured lights in a half-circle above his head. I had the knowledge that these were his guardian angels watching over him.

He was about four months old at the time. I have seen my daughter Charlie's angels whispering in her ear when she is playing on her own outside. This is when they appear to me to be bright white and take on the shape of a male or female adult human. Archangels are much larger than guardian angels and appear to me in human form with an aura of colour.

There are different angels for different jobs. Ask your guardian angels to wrap their wings around you; this is an angelic hug. The energy feels very peaceful. To hear your guardian angel's voice, you simply need to ask. You may not hear a voice as such; however, your guardian angels will leave a message to let you know they are around, either by signs or feelings. Angels will leave feathers for us to notice or a butterfly to greet us. I find this very regularly in psychic readings. A deceased loved one can also do the same; they will leave signs so that you know they are around and are just fine. Most people just know it is the angels or a loved one letting them know they are around. Anything that happens to you three or more times is a message from your angels.

The angels ask that you pay attention once you have asked for their help, so you will notice any signs they pop in your path or notice any feelings or ideas they may bring to you.

Your guardian angels have been assigned to one person—*you.* They are just waiting for you to ask them for help. As humans, we have the right to steer life the way we want, on our own if we choose. This is the law the angels work with: free will. The minute you ask for their help, they shine their light upon you to help you see the way.

One method I share with people is this: ask your guardian angel to hold your hand. Request your guardian angel to send you their healing energy. This is a very powerful way for people to connect with their own personal guardian angel, who is waiting to help them. When your angel touches your hand, it feels very much like a person holding your hand. When your angel begins to send healing energy, it will go up your arm and cover your entire body. Just bathe in this healing energy; only good will come of it. It feels very loving and peaceful, perhaps like nothing you have ever felt. I liken it to Reiki, which is a very gentle, loving energy.

This is very safe, and only your angels will hold your hand. If you do not feel anything, be assured that they are there with you. Sometimes when one feels unworthy of help or distrusts the angels, it may not work. Continue to ask your angels to hold your hand daily until you feel their loving touch.

Who Is My Guardian Angel?

As I mentioned earlier, angels have never incarnated on Earth and therefore have no egos. For this reason, they do not judge us. They love us unconditionally, just like a loving parent. They are not related to you, however; you may have the same angels from lifetime to lifetime. You choose these loving beings before you even come into this life—your guardian angel for your entire life.

Angels do have names, if you would prefer to use their names. Just ask them, and then look for any signs of an answer. Sometimes a name can be as simple as "Angel." Do not get too fixated on working out their name; the most important thing is to establish a relationship. They are happy to assist you in every way; all they would love in return is gratitude.

What Is a Guide?

A guide comes and goes throughout your life—depending on what you're going through—and can offer earthly advice. As they have walked the Earth, they understand what we are going through. Guides are more evolved than deceased loved ones. They are teachers and have done the extra study, as such, to be of service, learning how not to interfere with our free will. Guides may be family members, but this would not be recently deceased people, as they need time to heal themselves and go through lessons to learn to be a spirit guide. They have healing and a life review to complete first.

A guide is also present with children who have an imaginary friend. The guide will have an ego, as such, but will always be of service. Generally, but not always, you will not know the guide from this lifetime, but maybe from another lifetime.

A guide can also be an ascendant master, one who has reached enlightenment in his or her lifetime, such as Buddha, Jesus, or Mother Mary. If you have prayed and asked for help, this is when they come to you. Just as every angel has an area of expertise, so too do guides. God will send you the right one for the job.

Quite often, angels go through guides to talk or get messages to us. There is a reason for this. Imagine everything as being composed of energy; all matter is vibrating at either a slow or a fast rate. Angels vibrate very high and fast. As we have a body, we vibrate much slower than an angel. Those who have been on Earth also vibrate slower than an angel. Angels and guides need to slow down their vibration to talk to us, and in return, we need to lift our vibration to connect. So to get their message through to us, they will ask the guides to help. This is part of a guide's purpose, to give us the message of God. Guides also have a much more earthly approach, as they have walked the Earth and can have an understanding of what we are going through.

How Do I talk to My Angels?

Simply by having a chat with them, like you would any person! You may not hear or see them, but they are hanging on to every word you say. At the very moment you open your heart to them, they can then be a part of your life.

It is the law of free will that keeps many guardian angels unemployed. This law says that unless we ask for help, angels cannot intervene. The only exception to that law is if you are going to die before your time. The angels only then will intervene and save your life. So you see how safe you are; *nobody* dies until the right time and not a moment before. The right time is the time you choose before you come to earth. We are all here on earth to learn and grow. So before we are conceived, we choose up to three ages to leave earth.

Your angels simply wait and watch by your side until that very moment when you ask for help. Even if you're not very sure of what you want in life, just tell them everything, even though the angels already know all your secrets. You must first open your heart to them by telling them how you are feeling; this will allow them to have full access and begin the divine intervention. You have your own angels; they want to be a part of your life. If you are not asking for help, they are just hanging around doing nothing.

You may want to write a letter to your angels, simply telling them everything you are feeling. It may go like this:

Dear Angels,

Today I am feeling a little stressed. My kids are not cooperating, and the car has broken down. I have no money to get it fixed. Please help me!

Thanks, Angels
Love, me xx

The angels will talk to us through thoughts and feelings, so follow any feelings or repetitive thoughts in the coming moments or days. You may also see a sign, such as a licence plate, road sign, or other indicator. Prayers are almost never answered in the exact way we think they should be.

By simply saying, "Help me, please, angels," they can jump into action and make things happen. There is no right or wrong way to call on angels; the most important thing is to ask for help, and if you don't know what you're asking for, tell them that too.

I will give you some great examples of following guidance in the following chapters.

What if Someone Else Needs an Angel More?

Your guardian angels are for you and you alone! So you can never take help away from another person. The universe is abundant. Everyone has their own guardian angels. The reason I am writing this book is so every angel can get to work bringing peace to Earth one person at a time. What a loving place it would be if everyone knew there is no need to struggle! All we need to do is ask our angels. It would eliminate fear from the Earth. We would live in a world of peace, where the news would show only joy around the world.

Your own guardian angels are here just for you, so you can't take them from anyone else. The archangels are non-dimensional, which means they can be with more than one person at a time. They have a personal relationship with each and every one of us. There is an abundance of help in the universe.

What if I Do Not Deserve Help from the Angels?

Angels do not have egos; therefore, they do not judge you, but simply lend a hand. We all deserve help, no matter what we think we may have done wrong. Punishment serves no purpose; we learn and grow from mistakes.

The angels want us to know that there is no need to struggle. Life is meant to be joyous, and if a simple request, such as having a car park at the front door of the shopping centre, brings you peace, then please ask. Whenever I mention that you can ask your guardian angle to find you a car park at my platform shows, many people in the audience already know to ask the angels for a good car park and use this method regularly. It is just a simple request that brings so many of us peace. If you need more time or money, a new house or car, friends, health, or safety, just ask. The angels will happily assist you.

Anything is possible when we invite the angels into our lives. That is what the angels' purpose is, to bring us peace. I am very grateful for the angels in my life. I am in constant contact with them. My life goes from one strength to another; this would never have happened if I had not brought them into my life.

At first, I was hesitant to ask the angels for their assistance, especially for any more than one thing. I did not want to be greedy. But I grew to know that if the angels do not give direct intervention, they will guide us to make loving changes in our lives, which will bring more joy. They also taught me that the more I have, the more I have to give. When I feel joy, I pass this on to my children. I feel less stress when I have the bills paid and I have a day to myself. I then enjoy doing the household chores, as I feel more at peace, and I want to pass that on to everyone in my house.

What Do the Angels Want from Me?

All angels ever want in exchange for their help is a thank-you! Gratitude is their reward. The more grateful you are for all the things you have, the more you find to be grateful for. This gratitude brings the angels joy. They also want you to be happy and to spread the joy and laughter to all.

When you do a good deed for someone, if you are only looking for his or her gratitude, you did not seek something in return, just to know your love is appreciated. You know that if you give to someone and a thank-you is never given, you will eventually stop giving. The angels work the same way; they just want a thank-you.

Why Are My Angels Not Helping Me?

When we ask God or the angels for assistance, we simply need to tell them what the problem is and then get out of the way. The angels will take care of the rest.

Sometimes we think that if we ask for more money for food or clothes, we may win the lottery. The angels are more creative than that. You may find that someone drops by with a little extra food that they can't use or an outfit that no longer serves them but is just perfect for you. If you do not have an open mind, you may just have missed realizing that your prayer was answered. It rarely happens the way we think it should.

We have lessons to learn, and whether the lesson is to be more grateful or patient, everything happens in divine timing. That's not my favourite lesson; I like things to happen instantly, but I am a learning patience. I have learnt through a few speeding fines that when we force things to happen, we create blocks. When we just relax and go with the flow, things then happen quite quickly. The angels have shown me during healing sessions that God rushes nothing, and yet everything happens instantly.

Angels show us signs constantly as an answer to our prayers, so keep an eye out for this. They can come in many forms: TV, radio, billboards, numbers on clocks, or licence plates.

When my husband, Trent, and I were naming our fourth child, we were toying with the name Chase. I was on my way home from one of my psychic fairs, and a hotted-up green Ford sped up behind me. The car overtook me, and I instantly noticed on the licence plate the word CHASE. I knew it was a sign from the angels that this was the name our son wanted. I rubbed my belly and said, "Chase is your name." I got chills from the angels in confirmation that I was right. Chase was how the baby wanted to be known. The car sped off and was out of my vision within seconds. The angels are very creative, and we just need to be open to receiving. Any sign that appears in threes, take note. If you are not sure, ask the angels to show you again.

What Message Does My Angel Have for Me?

Your relationship with your angels is significant just for you. They will point you in the right direction, but please be patient, as they are just learning to work with you too.

If you do not understand your guidance or can't hear them, please just ask them to show you another way or to speak up. Please notice the repetitive thoughts and signs you see; anything that comes to you in threes is very important. This is a message to you from your angels.

Continue to pray and meditate frequently; this is how they can communicate with you better. Ensure that you spend time daily to relax (without alcohol) and take good, deep breaths. This is another way they can communicate with you.

You can never ask your angels for help too much. I am in constant contact with my angels, checking in with them throughout the day. Love and laughter are what they love you to have, so start talking to them now.

THE
ARCHANGEL MICHAEL

od has angels for every job, and in the "management department" are the archangels. Archangels are much bigger than guardian angels. These angels all have a particular job. I would like to introduce you to Archangel Michael.

Archangel Michael's aura is purple. You will know when he is around if you see purple angel lights out of the corner of your eyes. Extreme heat is another way Archangel Michael lets us know he is about. Michael's job is to rid the Earth of fear. He can do this in many ways. One of his many talents is to protect us from harm. Archangel Michael keeps us safe in the car, at home, on a plane, anywhere, anytime. His tasks can include removing lower energy from our home or office and showing us our true life's path and how to get on that path.

How Can He Be with More Than One Person at the Same Time?

The archangels can be with any number of people at any one time. The angels have a completely different and personal relationship with each and every one of us. It is only our limited beliefs that would have us think that this is not possible. As time is, in fact, non-linear as we perceive it, in fact everything is in the now. Archangels have no restriction by time and therefore can be anywhere, in any number of places.

Archangel Michael travels to school with each of my children. He lives in our home six times over, with each one of us. That's right—if you ask him, he will live with you. He is a very cheap guest. My children know that every time they are frightened, they can call on Michael to keep them safe. Archangel Michael is with me every time I do a psychic reading, and he keeps me safe from any lower beings.

Michael will work with you to find your divine life path and vacuum away any fears.

How Do You Vacuum Away Fears?

I credit the following healing to Doreen Virtue; it is her clear channel and her relationship with angels that have helped me along my journey. I use this method regularly and teach it to as many people as I can.

Take a few deep breaths and call on Michael by saying, "Archangel Michael, I call upon you now. Please bring your vacuum tube, and put the suction on high." Then imagine or feel him placing a vacuum pipe that is a bright white light on the top of your head, vacuuming any darkness from inside your body; going to every part of your body, to the tips of your toes and fingers, making sure to get all your organs. When he is finished, see or feel him flick the switch in reverse and fill all the space he just got rid of the darkness with a brilliant, white paste. You can also take this method to your aura and do the same.

During this process, you may feel energy shifts around the body. It can be similar to getting a Reiki treatment. You may feel very hot or see purple angel lights with both your psychical eye and your third eye. This is how Archangel Michael lets us know he is with us.

You can also use this vacuuming method with Michael and his band of mercy, his helping angels. As Michael's job is so large, he has many helpers. Simply request both Michael and his band of mercy to clear away any darkness from your home, office, school, shops, suburb, country, and Earth; the possibilities are endless.

You may also use this same method with your loved ones. I find it great to use on the children after school; it stops a lot of the crankiness and fighting amongst the children when they get in the car after school. When I walk through my daughter's kindy, I always ask Michael to vacuum the centre.

To use this method on a loved one, mentally ask his or her angels if they would like this. It is very rare for anyone to refuse when you are speaking to his or her higher self. Then picture or feel the vacuuming process being preformed on him or her in your mind's eye. This can be a very powerful experience.

What Else Can Michael Do?

Michael is limitless. He helps to purify our hearts of fear. Simply ask Michael to put his healing light around your heart. It is such a lovely feeling. If any thoughts, fears, or tears come up, please just let them out; allow yourself to cry. Michael will carry these lifelong burdens from you, especially those feelings you buried deep. It is only the fear of pain that stops us from releasing and moving forward. Nothing else holds us back like fear, and the Archangel Michael would like us to step out of this fear.

Michael keeps us safe from all harm. Many years ago, Michael saved my life and possibly my family's lives too. After an incident with an ex-partner, I hopped into the car and set off for the one place I would always feel safe: my parents' home. This time was different; I did not want to go there. Earlier, I had invoked the Archangel Michael for his protection. So when my heart chakra was yelling not to go there, I could not ignore it. My heart area was very hot, and when I focused on it, I knew the information was from him.

I just kept saying repeatedly, "I do not want to go to my parents' house." This made no sense to me. I had no idea where else to go or what else to do, so I just decided to drive around. While driving, my mobile phone rang; it was my mother telling me the ex had just been looking for me at their house, and he had a shotgun. Although my family were frightened and shaken, we are all still alive. I do not even want to think of what would have happened if I had been there. That was a life-changing experience. Thank you, Michael.

Michael is also to credit for plopping me on my divine life path. When guidance was given to take a course in Hawaii with Doreen Virtue almost halfway across the world, my instant thought was that I could not go over there on my own. As a mother of three, I felt a little guilty about leaving my children and their father, who is very supportive. It was my husband's idea for me to go on my own, as we did not have the money for all of us to go there. I procrastinated and asked Michael to let me know if it would be okay for me to go and if it was necessary. My husband continued to insist, and all I could think was that it would be five days away from them.

One night, I was awakened by a guardian angel sitting on the edge of my bed. I could feel his indentation in the bed. I saw him with my psychical eye, a bright, white male angel. His message was very clear and loud. He said "The children will be fine and safe. No emotional blockages would be caused from you going to Hawaii."

When I tried to ask a question, the angel asked me to be silent. He was there to give me the guidance I needed. His messages were very strong and very loving. I heard his voice very loudly inside my head. I felt reassured that travelling so far across the world was the right decision to make. The angel's presence was the answer to my prayers. It would bring me more clients to be of service to, just like I had been asking for. So I booked the course, flights, and accommodations the next day. I felt very nervous; however, knowing from previous experience that the angels are always right, I knew with all of me it was the right decision to make.

As my departure date drew nearer, I now had a new fear—of flying and crashing, leaving my children without a mother. My goodness, the ego will stop at nothing to keep us from joy!

In the coming weeks, I began to notice that our house was on a very busy flight path, as planes began waking me in the wee hours of the morning. I knew this was a message from the angels, showing me how many planes fly without crashing. I had never heard these planes before, and I do not hear them now. Flying continues to be much safer than being in a car. I thanked the angels for this insight, and I asked them to replace my fears with faith.

The day arrived when I had to kiss my children and husband good-bye. The children seemed fine with it. Their dad had lots of fun activities planned for when I was away. As I boarded the plane for Hawaii, the whole interior of the plane was purple; I was very excited, as this is Michael's colour. I knew I was going to be safe. I spoke to both him and the Archangel Raphael anytime I felt a little scared, asking them to replace my fears with faith. Michael and Raphael worked together with travel safety. Twenty-four hours later, I arrived safely at my destination.

The next morning, it was time for us to register for the course, and there were many people there from all over the world. I saw a number of books about the Archangel Michael on the registration table. I got excited, thinking, *Oh, we must all be getting a book,* but everyone in the line was walking away empty-handed. The girl in front of me enquired what the books were for. The administrator informed her that they were only for a randomly selected few. When it came time for me to register, I was handed the Archangel Michael book! I was very excited. Thank you, Michael! He never left my side the entire journey, from booking the tickets to helping rid me of fears along the way. He wanted me to know he is with me.

A few weeks after I returned home, my client based had not picked up to the point I had imagined. Michael had shown me in the days leading up to the course that lines of people would be waiting for me to do readings for them. This was not happening. So I meditated and said, "What more do you want me to do? I have followed all the guidance, and nothing has happened as I had seen." I felt disheartened and angry. Suddenly, my whole head went blank. I could feel Michael's energy; it was like the words were being pushed into the top of my head. I saw in my mind and heard the words *psychic fairs.* Instantly I knew I needed to start my own psychic fairs, and yet I doubted it. I rang a friend who, at the same time that night, was told she needed to start working in psychic fairs. I needed no further confirmation!

I got to work instantly. With Michael and many other angels by my side, this was the beginning of Selena Hill's

Psychic Fairs. My fairs are of service to light workers by providing a safe and uplifting environment for them to do their spiritual work. Selena Hill's Psychic Fairs provide authentic light workers for the general community and assist in healing and pointing people in the right direction.

Michael can give you the strength to do anything, and this includes getting on with your life's purpose. From the few insights I have given you, I have shown that his power is limitless and very grand. If you need guidance, strength, protection, or illumination from fear, the Archangel Michael will get you through.

THE
ARCHANGEL RAPHAEL

The next Archangel I would like to introduce to you is Raphael, the healing angel. Archangel Raphael has an aura of green. He works alongside of doctors, nurses, and anyone in the healing industry, especially light workers. Archangel Raphael works with his league of healing angels. They assist him in his healing work.

The Archangel Raphael will help you to heal when you are ill. You can ask Raphael to heal anyone who is sick. It is as simple as just requesting him to

Selena Hill

do so. You can pray to God and chat to the angels.

Raphael has a healing blanket that is green in colour, and you can ask him to wrap you or someone you care about in that blanket. Raphael and all the angels instantly respond to prayers for children. Sometimes when we call upon our angels for help, human actions are required. One night I lay next to my nine-week-old baby when he had a cough. I knew instantly it was croup. I began praying to God and invoking the Archangel Raphael and his healing angels. I asked if he could instantly heal my baby. I had Chase in bed with us, and he wanted to feed. As I put him on my breast, he could not feed and breathe. I got a massive feeling telling me to get into a hot shower with him. I had my husband get the phone and ring the after-hours doctor, asking him to come to us, only to discover that they do not come to our area.

I got another number from them, which was for a nurse. I was in the bathroom, which was full of steam. I sat under the heat lamp with him feeding. The nurse heard my baby and said he was struggling to breathe. The nurse summoned an ambulance and began giving me directions on putting him in a steamed room to wait for the ambulance. Of course, I was already there. The ambulance was at our home within ten minutes, and his struggle to breathe was not as severe by the time the ambulance got to us. We arrived at the hospital, where he was given a mild steroid and enough for three days. We had an overnight stay in hospital as a precaution, but he was fine.

The angels always respond quickly when we or a loved one is in danger. When my firstborn son, Ethan, was just walking, he was about nine or ten months old. We were feeding a horse as a part of our daily routine, in a paddock right behind my children's play area. The children's play area was a meter higher than the horse's paddock. There was a wire fence that the horse would poke his head through and eat the grass as he watched the kids. This horse was a "kid-friendly pony," so I was assured by the owner, a horse enthusiast and friend.

My children were playing as usual. I was a meter from them, sweeping the patio. The next thing I knew, in front of my eyes, my baby was being picked up by his hand in the mouth of the horse. I yelled, *"Angels, help!"* I heard the word *scream,* so as loud as I could, I let out a powerful, protective, motherly scream. The horse dropped him immediately and ran away.

His little baby hand was marked and beginning to swell. "Archangel Raphael, please help!" I said aloud. I had a strong feeling to put my hand around his and give it Reiki, and Raphael showed me his green healing light around Ethan's hand. Ethan settled down instantly.

Within about five minutes, my son began to wriggle, as he wanted down. I removed my hands from his. Ethan's hand looked as though nothing had happened, not even an indentation where the horse's teeth had been. The swelling was completely gone! Ethan hopped up and began playing. We stayed away from the horse from that day forward. No extra carrots for that horse! I am very grateful this was an instant miracle.

Sometimes we can ask for assistance, and it may not happen. Once, just after I had been in a car accident, I came out without a scratch, until later that evening. When I went to bed, I could hardly move. Of course, I shed a few tears and felt a little sorry for myself, like people do. I asked Raphael and Michael for some healing, and nothing seemed to be happening, so I asked again. But still nothing seemed to happen.

I had learnt, though, that you sometimes need to put your foot down to the universe when you are requesting something. So in a forceful but loving voice, I said, "I know you can heal me instantly. I have no need for this pain. Take it away now!" I said it with such determination that I instantly felt the presence of Raphael and Michael, and they began the healing. I could feel them extract the pain from my body. I went on to have a peaceful night's rest, waking without any pain.

Raphael also can help us to heal all addictions. We simply need to pray and ask Raphael to help us to realise that we no longer need caffeine, drugs, cigarettes, alcohol or anything else we no don't want. He can help us to crave healthy food and drinks. He will also help us to lose weight healthfully and keep it off. All you need to do is ask.

Archangels can also do instant healings. When I was dating my husband, Trent, he was constantly suffering from leg cramps. One night, when Trent was again in pain, I asked in my mind if the Archangel Raphael could help him. Raphael responded, "Get his permission." I heard this statement very clearly.

I was a little reluctant, as at the time we had only been dating a short time. He knew I was psychic and I did Reiki and angel healings. However, I had not shared any angel messages with him, let alone a healing. I had complete faith that if Raphael had asked for his permission, a great healing would occur.

I began by telling Trent the angels would like to heal his cramps, but they need his permission. "Sure, I'll give anything a go," he responded.

I was over the moon. I very much wanted to be in a relationship where I could be my true self. I then asked him to say, "Angels, I give you permission to heal my cramps. Thank you." He repeated this statement. Raphael worked on him instantly. Trent was sleeping within a few minutes. My soon-to-be husband did not get another cramp, nor has he had another one since. Of course, now he believes in angels; he had no idea about angels before, and now he knows they do exist. It still amazes him, and yet he now has more than that to be grateful for from the angels. He supports me in my light-worker's journey, one I could not do without him.

Raphael is the healing angel. He works alongside Archangel Michael, at times to help heal and repair the work of lower energies. He will also keep you safe during travel, alongside Michael. Raphael is always in my healing room, guiding my hands and words to those who need healings. Raphael provides healing to anyone who asks. There is no right or wrong way to request his help, but as you have seen from my husband's healing, it is important that you do ask.

MORE MIRACLES

There is no limit to how the angels can help you and those you love. When life throws its toughest times at you, you sometimes can't see for looking. This is when the angels can see from the inside out and help get you out of the mess you created.

When I split from my first husband, I had two small children. I was feeling very guilty about them not having a father and doubted if I had made the right decisions. Even though this man had threatened my life and my family's lives, I still believed—or wanted to believe—that his being in rehab was the answer to my prayers.

I no longer felt any love towards this man, but I held him close to my heart, as he was the biological father of my first two children. Like many who stay in an unhappy and unstable environment, I wanted my children to have both parents. I was also worried about how society would view me as a single mother. Every night when my two babies were sleeping, I would sit in the middle of their room and pray.

As I sat, I invited all our guardian angels into the room—mine, my children's, and my ex's. I ask them to help me make the right decision for both of the children. I just wanted them to grow up in a loving, safe environment. Day by day, I got stronger and stronger. It got to the point where I knew that this relationship was not right for any of us. The angels helped me to see the truth by removing fear. I finally got the strength to move out on my own with the children; however, he tried to pull on my heartstrings. The angels held my hand every day. Still I constantly doubted that I had made the right decision.

One night as I feel asleep, I saw in my mind's eye my son Ethan. He grabbed my hand and took me outside our home. In my vision, he pointed up to the sky. I had no idea what he was trying to tell me. I said, "I do not know what you are trying to say. What do you want to tell me?" I then saw in my mind's eye, my daughter walking toward us.

She said, "He wants you to listen to God, Mummy. We do not like our daddy."

With that, the vision ended. I cried myself to sleep that night. I awoke in the morning, knowing I had to stay strong. In my vision, I could feel the emotions behind my children's message. This vision gave me a complete knowingness, and I felt very free and happy when I awoke in the morning.

Now on my own, young and not wanting to spend my life alone, I had a new prayer. I again sat in my children's rooms and talked to their angels. Every night I asked to meet a guy who would love and treat my children as if they were his own. I also included list of requirements I desired in a partner. Six months passed before my prayers were answered, a *long* six months.

One day I saw Trent. We had dated a few times towards the end of high school. Trent had been a couple of grades above me. We had mutual friends in high school and would regularly catch up at parties. We also went to a few concerts together. Nothing ever eventuated, as I was looking for a serious relationship, and Trent just wanted to have fun with his mates. I remember my dad saying to my mother on one of Trent's many visits, "She'll end up marrying him."

When my dad made that statement, I just knew I would. I was about fifteen or sixteen at the time and never gave this much thought. We had not seen each other for about a decade. Trent was walking towards me at the local shopping centre. This had been the hangout place when we were teenagers. I moved back to the area when I split from my ex.

When I saw Trent, I had the strongest butterflies in my tummy, and I swear the angels pushed the word *hello* out of my mouth. He instantly recognised me. The first thing he asked me was if I was still with that guy. "No, I am single," I replied, letting him know I was available. He asked me if the two little ones in front of me were mine. He said they were cute and he loved kids. We chatted a little longer and then went our separate ways. I was kicking myself that I did not take his number or offer my own. I went home and began to look on a dating site, thinking I had missed my chance with Trent. There he was—the first guy who was on the screen. I could not believe it! I sent him an e-mail and waited for a reply.

The following day, a friend and I were off to the Gold Coast for the Indy, a large annual car-racing event. She is psychic also and had said to me a couple of weeks previous that she had no idea why, but we needed to be at the Indy. Trusting her messages, I was along for the ride. We had only been at the Indy for a few hours when I saw Trent sitting by himself. We smiled and began to chat. My loving friend ensured that phone numbers were exchanged. He said that he had wanted get my number earlier and he thought he had missed his chance. I gave him my number. I cleverly thought that if he was truly interested, he would call, and my friend had not forced him to take my number. I knew why it was so important for us to be there. Trent and I had met up three times in a matter of a few days so I would know that it was a sign from my angels. *Was he my soul mate?*

Two weeks passed, and I had not received a call from Trent. I had gone over the whole scenario a few times. *It's been three times within a few days; surely it was meant to be.* It was all the signs the angels had taught me. Just as I had given up hope, my phone rang. It was him! One of the first things I said was, "Why did you take so long to ring?" It turns out he had been in hospital, quite ill. So I guess that was one of those "being patient" things.

Our first date was a great success; we spent the whole night chatting. We made arrangements to catch up in a few days. Our relationship continued to grow and blossom. He built a wonderful relationship with the kids; Trent was all they talked about. We had lots of outings with the children and spent hours in the back yard, playing together. My children had never experienced a complete family before. I had been the only one taking on both father and mother roles their entire lives. Every time Trent arrived, they would run to greet him.

After a while, in the natural progression of the relationship, it came time for Trent to move in with us. I chatted with the children about him moving in with us, and my daughter, who was three at the time, was very excited and said, "We now have a family."

Charlie wrapped her arms around me and was jumping with joy. She asked me if they could call Trent *Daddy*. I replied, "If it is okay with him, then it is okay with me." I had never seen her so happy.

That night, Trent came over when the kids were already in bed. I let him know what Charlie had said earlier in the day. He was instantly thrilled with the idea, and I even saw a tear. This is what I had been asking for in my prayers; I was feeling very grateful and content. The next day, when Trent arrived home after work, the kids ran out, as they always did, and Charlie asked him instantly if they could call him *Daddy.* Trent cuddled her into his arms and whispered that he would love that. Now married, we have added another two children to the mix.

I am very grateful to the angels that I have a truly fantastic marriage. He ticks all the boxes, and he shares every part of parenthood with me. From the cleanup of vomit to the first day of school, he is always there. I enjoy his company every day and want to come home to him. We laugh and play together. He is my best friend and the father of all four of my children.

KIDS AND ANGELS

Children have a natural connection with angels, as their visions and thoughts have not been distorted. Children are very sensitive in picking up on the energy, because their hearts are not as heavy as adults'; nor are their minds and bodies burdened with stress. Their bodies are light, and therefore it is easy to hear, feel, see, or know their angels' messages. Children's guardian angels are quite often a child's imaginary friend. As angels are a huge part of our lives, all my children have been taught about the angels. They know which angel to call on for what they need at the time.

One time, my daughter Charlie was in the school talent show. She wanted to win second place, since the prize was free tuckshop. Charlie and I asked her angels to help. She came in second and won her free tuckshop. Charlie always talked to her angels and had complete faith that they would help her. She still passes on their words of wisdom to other like-minded people.

My son Ethan lost his very expensive school hat. So he and I asked the Archangel Michael and the Archangel Chamuel (who finds lost things) to find Ethan's hat and return it to us. To our surprise, a few weeks passed and still no hat. Ethan got a new school hat. The next school year, about six months after we asked for the angels to find the hat, it was handed to Ethan at school. This reminded us that we must let them know everything we want to happen.

When one wants to become a mother and it is just not happening, the Archangel Gabriel is the angel you can call on. When I was trying to conceive my fourth child, it did not happen for the first two months, so I called on her for help. We conceived the next month.

I see the Archangel Gabriel as female. She works with parents wanting to conceive and with parenting issues. Some know Gabriel to be male. The angels, in truth, have no gender. They are not male or female; they simply take on an energy that is right for their job. I know Gabriel to be a mothering angel. I have done healing on both myself and clients, and she always comes to me as female. As angels have no ego, it would not bother them either way.

I have seen clients who have been trying to conceive for years. I've quite often found that guilt, fear of childbirth, stress, and other related elements have been the reason why people have not conceived for five or even ten years. These people have been through many IVF treatments with no success. I have gone on to do healings with the Archangel Gabriel and let people know that she is the one that helps with conception.

One of my clients, who had been trying to conceive for five years with a number of IVF treatments, conceived within one month of a healing with me invoking the Archangel Gabriel, channelling a healing with her during the two Reiki sessions.

The angels show me that fear keeps one from moving forward. Some individuals are like an animal in the headlights of an oncoming car, unable to move in any direction. Fear robs people of joy and constantly blocks miracles. Therefore, fear will stop our heart's desires from reaching God. Sometimes we do not even realise that we have these fears.

To remove such fears in pregnancy, it is as simple as calling on the Archangel Gabriel. She will help you to recognise these fears and help you to let go. Remember, all that is required is for you to ask. I have written a meditation with the Archangel Gabriel to help people to conceive naturally. It is available to purchase on my website and at Selena Hill's Psychic Fairs.

Angels always want to help children. A concerned mother brought her son to see me after they had been to many doctors and counsellors. He had been having toileting accidents since his parents' separation; the child was embarrassed, and the mother was at the point of desperation.

As I was speaking to the mother over the phone, the angels instantly showed me the fears the young boy was dealing with and how I could be of service. After one visit with the child and the mother, an instant healing occurred. I have a written testimony from the young man's mother on how, after just one visit—a combined Reiki and angel healing—he is a different boy and no longer having toileting accidents.

The angels are the ones who conducted these healings. I am the facilitator. Full credit goes to the angels for the above miracles. I am merely showing you how quickly and easily the miracles occur. You do not need to have any qualifications; you simply need to be open to receiving and ask them for help. I would like to say again that there is no right or wrong way to invoke them; it is as simple as having a conversation or writing a letter.

This healing has brought both mother and son peace, and that is the angels' purpose: to bring peace on Earth one person at a time.

There are archangels that specifically work with children, including the Archangel Metatron. He helps children, particularly those with ADD and ADHD. He will help parents seek alternatives to drugs for children diagnosed with these disorders. I have found a lot of children given this label are quite sensitive to energy and are easily distracted by other entities or lower energies, especially in classroom situations. There are a lot of energies put together in one room.

Using the cleansing and protecting techniques in the Archangel Michael chapter can make a huge difference to children's behaviour. Food also has a massive impact on a child's behaviour. Try this yourself: exclude sugar from your diet for a few days, and then drink a can of soft drink. It is a major sugar hit and can make you quite jittery and give you a high amount of excess energy.

Children's bodies are smaller than ours. When they are bombarded with sugary foods, they are on a constant high. They are not at a maturity level to sit still or deal with this feeling; instead, they act out.

Archangel Metatron also will help adults wanting to pursue a career helping children. Just ask him, and he will steer you in the right direction.

Archangel Gabriel works with parents and parenting issues. She will help and guide parents when they are struggling to know how to help their children. This angel can give you an inner nudge and ideas that can help during those sleepless nights with babies. I have asked her many times for help with all of my children. She will give me an idea to help put a young one to sleep during teething, such as wrapping a baby tightly or rocking him or her in a pram. The Archangel Gabriel has also given me the strength to be strong and firm with babies when nothing is wrong with them, such as weaning them off of nighttime feeds.

Of course, all the archangels will help children. These are just the ones who specialise in parenting or children's problems. If you're ever stuck and unsure of which angels to ask for, a general prayer will bring you the right angels to help you.

THANK YOU, ANGELS

I experience angel blessings every day. The more you chat to your angels, the easier life gets, and life turns great quickly. When things do not go the way I want, I look inwards to see what I need to heal. By constantly healing, letting go, and forgiving, it gets easier and easier to hear the angels' messages for me. I have not always been able to hear the messages as clearly as I can today. This has come from many life lessons. Learning to trust my own intuition has been a big one. I see this constantly in many psychic readings I do. If people listen to what their guts are saying, they would seldom be in the bind they are in.

It is my hope that by letting you into my life to share the miracles that angels have created for me constantly, you too will spend time chatting with your angels. The angel miracles that I have shared with you are the ones that have made big and lasting changes in my life. I have so many more that I have not even begun to touch the surface. You deserve to have a life of joy and peace, even if you are not aware of it yet.

From my experience, I wanted to let you know that no matter where you are in your life, you can receive guidance, love, and protection from the angels. All you need to do is ask, and the miracles will flow. You do not need to be a psychic or a priest or have never made a mistake. They love all of us, and they are here to help. They love you unconditionally for who you are right now. You simply need to ask and invite the angels into your life.

There is no right or wrong way to communicate with the angels. Just make sure you do.

Love, light, and angel blessings.

— Selena Hill

ABOUT THE AUTHOR

Selena Hill is a psychic medium and Reiki master/teacher. She is the founder of Selena Hill's Psychic Fairs and co-founder of Psychic Fairs Spiritual Learning Centre. Both have been created to help nurture light workers and those needing help and direction. Selena has been passing information from angels, guides, and deceased loved ones since 2005. She currently runs a number of workshops on spiritual development, Reiki, and children's Reiki, and holds regular shows in which she gives messages from above. You can find out more about Selena at *www.psychicfair.info.* Selena lives in Queensland, Australia, with her husband, Trent, and their four children.

NOTES

NOTES

NOTES